TARTARUS

Tartarus

poems by

Ty Chapman

Button Publishing Inc.
Minneapolis
2024

TARTARUS
POETRY
AUTHOR: Ty Chapman
COVER DESIGN: Zoe Norvell

◇

ALL RIGHTS RESERVED

© 2024 by Ty Chapman

◇

Published by Button Poetry
Minneapolis, MN 55418 | http://www.buttonpoetry.com

◇

Manufactured in the United States of America
PRINT ISBN: 978-1-63834-084-3
EBOOK ISBN: 978-1-63834-086-7
AUDIOBOOK ISBN: 978-1-63834-085-0

First printing

For my dear mother who made me the man I am.
For my mentors & collaborators who made me the artist I am.
For my friends, family, & loves who bring meaning to life.

Contents

TARTARUS

GOD SAY (BIG G)

You swing
still blackened fruit
crucifix burned beneath
abundant prayers never heard
I thought we made it clear
your kind won't find
home here

TARTARUS

After Jean-Michel Basquiat

[Victor]
Such a lengthy tumble to fall from god's good grace,
from upper planes on down to Tartarus. Our wings clipped,
feet full of scoria. Something lusts in umbras—entities
we cannot name. Such endless descension,
slaughtering scores for spiteful ideals. Snapping bones
& gnashing prongs, a dissonance heard for miles.

[Cabra]
Deep beneath each ring of hell
exists a place innominate to all.
A land so calamitous & cold,
even Virgil would think twice
before tour-guiding. In its center,
a long black desk collaged with
catalogues & well-crossed items.
Satan's pale hands go about
harvesting Kings from on high.
An endless gluttony.

[Six Crimee]
Bright-eyed angels decorate the old hood
where halos get artisanally crafted. Handmade
with malice, the hollow points burrowing
within our holiest sites across from the playground
where they scotch-hop with hollowed casings;
the sandbox overflowing—so many toothless remains.

[Bird on Money]
King hops through the chaos of U.S. A trepid
prospect for one so small, but King knows well
the bridleways death wanders. He hops along to
inaudible frequencies, foraging misplaced
morsels.

& he don't hurt nobody
& he don't live grand
& he don't hurt nobody
& he don't live long.

[Mecca]
What quaint Arcadia—see the way
a city can fit snugly in your palm. Its rough edges
protruding just so. Idyllic
from a distance—the cacophony of war machines lost
in the gentle wafting breeze. See here, a slice of Elysium,
safety with a rooftop view. Think not on the horrors below.
Hear not the wails of the damned.

[World Crown]
King was trapped at birth
in a well-lit arena; far beneath
jeering onlookers, he throws hands
with Death. From genesis,
he's been taught to dodge
jabs. A million missed connections.
But fighters know a simple truth:
you only need to slip up once
to join his aggregation.
They say it is ever expanding.

DOWNFALL'S THEME

Listen to that soft melody in the air
how it underscores the daily mill & trill
but don't give no comfort
ain't no Negro song
it don't got no beat ain't neat but sound familiar
like so many skinheads raging in the street
like fork-tongued devils in different 'fits
but monstrous all the same
it sounds like a sort of downfall
the volume wanes to trick niggas into guessin'
the record dun quit spinnin'
but we know it never does
'cause the moment you turn them pretty cheeks
the racket swells again
that soft discordant tune that lacks soul
& feels at home in ours as much as a horror   as a gunman
lurking by the cracked basketball courts   gripping a tin badge
or beside a church bursting at the plaster with niggas
listen how it never really wavers
how the kid-kin hooping out back have learned
to twostep to its awful cadence   to sample the sound
& make something pretty   how   the song is so familiar
we know it better than our neighbors
how it burdens chests & shoulders
& we know
where the baseball bats be   but no one
smashes the   goddamned   record
so it loops   & listen

listen to that soft melody in the air

FUCK THE HASTAG IN YOUR TINDER BIO

trending, then forgotten. trending, then forgotten.

PANTHEON

The spirit aches most days—
immense bloodcost of godhood.
Our ichor free-flowing
       fresh from the spigot,
Black alluring to wayward gazes.
How it pains to know they held us once
as prophets:
       pockets overflowing,
       relics & riches.

How quiet burns
       as necks meet concrete
       or more traditional means.
How it rages to know
we've given everything
& still ain't seen a cent.
Overseers' children still relish Black
sweat so long as it's free.

~

My city / not-home
bursting at the pavement
with bloodlust hunters;
so much roaming rabble,
walking tantrums with
automatic armaments.
Yeah, yeah,
but more-so the city,
its different factions & all
their twisted   instruments—
guns & germs & steel—
       sure.
But also the stares

of America's initiates—
cushy cult built on
            unwilling offerings—
the way a stranger might
gaze & see something sub-
human. Wounded beast in clothes,
flesh-mess fit for the altar.
Their mutterings:
            You poor thing
            you don't even see
            the knife coming.
It's cool tho', 'cause
I got legions behind me:
            sisters & brothers
            wacky uncles & elders
who go back, like, four flats & all that.
The ones who seen pain's shifting faces,
enough to know nuance.
The way it runs a visage rugged.

The ones who offer a warm embrace,
            or a hand,
                        or a fifth
to ward against the wicked.

O, how we fountain of youth at functions;
the spring of sameness washing our
            shimmering   onyx.
How we rise each day,
pulleyed by bootstraps,
& still ain't welcome.

            Knee on neck,
                        face on pavement;
            all he wanted
                        was his momma.
                                    To be held

& know in his whole body
he'd be all right.

I know I'm meant to drop
        to knees & praise
caucasian savior's name
'cause a killer's locked away.
You'd have me shuck & jive,
            wail & cry,
as you mutter:
            You poor thing.
Your daily deed a three-minute sampling
of pain—but I can't go out like that.
These scars ain't open for tourism,
this Black not yours to pity.
Not when *justice* is a Contigo in the Pacific,
& the blue wave crashes endless—every day.

Our seaside palisades
a far cry from safety
beneath your elevated estates.
Ain't no *kumbaya* 'til all
the rivers run dry. The oceans drained.

All he wanted was his momma.

Don't speak to me of justice
while my people in shackles
        & graves
for getting mouths fed
        & bills paid,

while your balding dog of war
might yet feel the light of day,
the grass beneath his feet,
the way the birds sing regardless

of which war crime took place today.

IN MINNEAPOLIS

I learned at a very young age
to stay my ass inside
hiding from
the spindle-limbed
steady-reaching officers of the
laws I always seem to break
not always intentionless
but no one told me there was rules
against walking outside to feel
the sun balm my cheeks
while humming a song
that burned
a hole in my chest
teetering
on a cement wall
just to see if I could maintain this
uneasy sway
without kissing sidewalks
but when downtown
by the business folks
walking in tight-assedly
from the 'burbs
there *was* such a law
& when the officer caught me
far from classes I should've been in
bouncing along to whatever tune
I had certainly cranked to 100
he barked something inaudible
which I came to realize was
get down from there
& me being young
& distractable
& maybe a little too bold
off some fresh Creator's chant
I asked a question

figuring it was sensible
& not at all
a deathwish
I asked
why
& his tone dropped like
it too was reaching for a pistol
& he growled
because I said so
& there was a sort of
venom dripping from his
thin lips which curled
as if they'd known the taste
of something rancid
perhaps twitching
half-dead in the street
& there on that wall
I thought of Trayvon
who was then freshly
reduced
to a hashtag
by an amateur
with cop-dreams
repeating what he saw
on TV maybe
boots on streets & throats like mine
& I learned
still young
to watch them folk
who equate safety to a gun
because them be the ones
to kick in your door
& pour an extended clip
into your still-falling chest
I learned that some people's
idea of protection is six feet of soil
between you & open air

& your momma's tears falling
to nourish what blooms from your ribcage
& while I'm too stubborn a buck
to stop asking why
I learned
in parts of the city
it's best to not be seen
lest I'm labeled a problem
solved in nine seconds

LET ME BE CLEAR—I'M AFRAID

I might linger too long
in unmoving air,
stale as muck-lined lakes,
huffing slate smoke
off the lips of another.
I fear I'm not planning
to leave this place behind,
this hate made famous
for bodies it breaks.
Land of countless corpses,
all plucked & colored strange.
Ivory poplar gnarled,
stretching zaftig roots
past any bed I'd wish
to dream within, constricting
Earth's innards & mine.
& I'm not planning to leave
this time. I feel it in my core,
the aches & burdens of prey
well-shadowed, how the building burn
laps my nape, knowing
why gazes linger, that this
land will soon split wide,
& I'll tumble to a tomb
I never hoped to rest in.
& by the time I clock
ghostly limbs descending,
it will already be too late.

PHILOPHOBIA: AN HEIRLOOM

Here he is—another fatherless son,
ever-clouding away like a drift.

Clouding away like that's all love is;
slushing through the assonance of lifeblood.

Assonance of lifeblood like a war drum, he say
wait for eye-whites, ready to kill like he done it before.

Wait for the kill like he done it before.
Well-traveled hitman—a boy like his father,

well-traveled, like his father, he smell arrows in flight.
Know six-milly ways to dodge one,

six-milly ways to say *I don't love you*,
like dying with two kids & a bastard.

Like dying without telling the son of the bastard.
There he is—another fatherless son.

CONFESSIONS OF A BASTARD

For L.C.

I never knew you would tower so, meeting pilots
with a smile so radiant they emergency landed

by the mall, where we met outside Panda Express,
just a jog from the sports bar we named ~~middle ground,~~

refuge to shit-talk & flex our war wounds,
to make up for eternities lost at the start of a gun.

I remember, still, the flame of rebellion welling up inside
my bird-bone chest—to think, my own father was a

fan of the Lakers. I remember, still, your dismay to know
I rocked a pink polo thinking I was some has been rapper,

but you hid it well enough; the conversation didn't fizzle
'til I finally worked up the insolence to rest my elbows

on the table & meet your gaze like a man to ask why,
after 16 years, you weren't around. & you

took it on the chin & explained, & it's no one's business
but ours, so what were we if not family? I think I finally learned

how to love you there as you guffawed & bellowed,
lifting cloth to brandish scars from heart surgery like

they were a badge of honor or perhaps the funniest things a human had
conceived, & much later—when I was a frightful man myself,

also laughing at ill-mending lesions—it clicked
that you, Father, were a holy man who believed in honeyed concepts

like *heart failure* existing within clockwork.
The machinations of a sadistic tinkerer. I

think it brought you comfort & wisdom. Perhaps
that's why our summit was such a sudden necessity.

& so long as we're getting right with god—
before the end, I mean—you should know that

when I was young, I stole Pokémon toys from
the kid who bullied me because I could, because

Hypno is cool as shit; so long as you don't Google
his origins. I've always held grudges,

been prone to fits of sorrow, not very effective at
saying goodbye, which is why I once wished death

would haunt your stoop. Again—when I was young.
& I think I mostly didn't want your other family to

have you either. I've never been one to bite tongues
or turn cheeks; but, like you, I've learned to say, *I was wrong. I didn't know.*

I didn't know farewell in the parking garage would be goodbye,
not 'til I was wrapped in my mother's arms. I was told you passed

peacefully, in bed with someone you loved, which is all one can hope for.
If I knew, I'd have asked for a single picture

or at least a knowing handshake. Like you, I see
Death around the corner, dripping lust from every orifice it can,

fiending to add a Chapman to the list, & I'm afraid
I'll go before telling you I'm sorry.

As the Texas sun dips, setting a chill
on Southern breezes, kicking dirt in my eye

that's entirely too red—the dirt, I mean—I wonder
if it's related to the scores of family

resting just beneath it. I went to your grave once
when no one was around. I left a stone atop

yours. & now, a frightful man, writhing in the dark
to melancholy 808s, I wonder if it's still there;

if my love for you can be evidenced.

Or if it too is lost, somewhere South, with all my missing loves.

DAD HAD FOUR KIDS, THREE OF WHICH WERE PRECIOUS

[Dad] ▪▪▪▪▪▪▪▪▪▪ passed away ▪▪▪▪▪▪▪▪▪▪ 2011 ▪
▪▪▪▪▪▪▪▪▪▪▪▪ was born ▪▪▪▪▪ 1969 ▪▪▪▪
▪▪▪▪▪▪▪▪▪▪▪▪▪▪▪▪▪ in ▪▪▪▪ TX. ▪
▪▪▪▪▪▪▪▪▪▪▪▪▪▪▪▪▪▪▪▪

▪▪▪▪▪▪▪▪▪▪▪▪▪▪▪▪▪▪▪▪
▪▪▪▪▪▪▪▪▪▪▪▪▪ his mother ▪▪▪▪
▪▪ raised him as a single parent ▪▪▪

▪▪▪▪▪▪▪▪▪▪▪▪▪▪▪▪▪▪▪▪
▪▪▪▪▪▪▪▪▪▪▪▪▪▪▪▪▪▪▪▪
▪▪▪▪▪▪▪▪▪▪▪▪▪▪▪▪▪

▪▪▪▪▪▪▪▪▪▪▪▪ he held various ▪▪▪
▪▪ company with his efforts culminating to ▪▪
▪▪▪▪▪▪▪▪▪▪▪▪▪▪▪▪▪▪
▪▪▪▪▪▪▪▪▪▪▪▪▪▪▪▪▪
▪▪▪▪▪▪▪▪▪ Tracks left behind ▪▪▪
▪▪▪▪▪▪▪▪▪▪▪▪▪▪▪
▪▪▪▪▪▪▪▪▪▪▪▪▪ an inspiration
to others.
▪▪▪▪▪▪▪▪▪▪▪▪▪▪▪▪▪▪
▪▪▪▪▪▪▪▪▪▪▪▪▪▪▪▪▪▪
▪▪▪▪▪▪▪▪ His was a world of ▪▪▪
▪▪▪▪▪▪▪▪▪▪▪▪▪▪▪▪▪▪
▪▪▪▪▪▪▪▪▪▪▪▪ cherished ▪▪
▪▪▪▪▪▪▪ children ▪▪▪▪▪▪▪
▪▪▪▪▪▪▪▪ his favorite ▪▪▪▪
▪▪▪▪▪▪▪▪▪▪▪▪▪▪▪▪▪▪
▪▪▪▪▪▪▪▪▪▪ children; ▪▪▪
▪▪▪▪▪▪▪▪▪▪▪▪▪▪▪▪▪

He is survived by his

son and best buddy,
daughter and precious princess,
son, Ty

and his precious Yorkshire
Terrier

SO, THERE WAS THIS DOG

tied to a tree behind an old fixture—
not dated like all East Side buildings, like rundown,
decrepit, indifference as tradition, a lonely thing, unkempt.
Like the dog with matted fur, snarling & champing
on the chain link fence—futile erosion, condemnation.
This beast,
     all bloodshot,
                filth,
        malice,
                    fear,
                        & I
had a recurring appointment. Each brisk jaunt to the bus stop
met with a proclamation across the fence. Each sunrise,
after *Grim Adventures* & Apple Jacks, came a sensory assault walk.
That bombardment
    of barks
      & scarfing wind,
        lunging at this
            gate
we both knew
    could be   cleared
without much   fuss   or trouble.
                  But
chained
    as he was,
          I had   no reason
                 to flee,   as I did
                 to the other side
                 of the street
                 where this mangy
                 reaper seemed less
                 a threat & mostly
                 distant,
                 a minor

                                        inconvenience,
                                  & a little pitiful,
                                    & not at all

              Death's visage
                    on four legs.

I still think of across-the-fence
& the fence & the dog & the house
which held my would-be killer,

& I figure each lacked love.
For what hound is birthed thirsting
for anything but nourishment?

              Who chooses cruelty if not for life? For fear?
              What dog who hasn't known a steel-toed kiss
                    goes looking to bite?

                    & yes, the dog is a metaphor,
                    & of course it's a vehicle for
                    the hate we have to give, but

                          meet me
                          at the
                          gate;

                          I'm not
                          done
                          speaking

of the dog
who thirsts
so wholly
for refuge
it lunges

at whomever
throttles
its allotted
solitude.

      this creature, which
       learned a single tactic
      to keep aggressors at bay—

        meet me
        at the
        gate—

    who hasn't known a steel-toed kiss?
    Bloodied knuckles & echoes
    so foul we keep them thickly chained

in the backyard
without sustenance,
praying they'll perish
by nightfall

            with our hands
             unbloodied
           thoroughly trimmed
        free of ~~callous~~ callus.

    & who hasn't been
    the chained animal,

all spittle & tooth,
to keep aggressors at bay?

        meet us
        at the
        gate.

If I had those
mornings to attempt again,
I would not hold my killer close
nor go running to embrace it,
but I wouldn't run away.

I'd inch close
as I could,
meeting face-to-face
each sunrise to offer
a smile without malice.

I'd meet
him at
the gate.

Knowing too well
why he lunges,

what he longs for
when no one is around.

ADRIFT

The Milky Way contains over one-hundred billion stars.
Between them lies the endless cold. The ever-dark.

The last beautiful thing. & within that empty lies
an ocean of detritus. The forgotten clutter.

That's where you'll find me. Floating
in this cosmic pond; a pod of paltry particles.

What are the odds? Floating here
of all places? So, in your presence,

the light is all I know. Your brilliance blinding.

I, too small—too lost at sea to remain tethered.

TARTARUS

After Jean-Michel Basquiat

[Man With Horns]
When does the man
fighting for survival's sake cease
to be himself? His hands made pale
from well-struck punches. Sifting through
catalogues, crossing items with vehemence.
How long can we play their games
until their horns are ours to claim?
& once we've donned infernal garb,
how long 'til hunger has its way?

[Fishing]
Some days, King plays god by the edge
of the lake. Reeling life at random—
King be such cruel arbiter. Flexing his callous
as waves crash gently. He leaves his victims
swinging 'neath the flame, & he don't stop
hauling 'til god rests their weary luster.

As tides begin to creep, King drops low,
whispers to his centennial kill. He says,
Better you than me.

[Pork Sans]
King's crown is full of thoughts dark
as tar. The type that creep up slow over
years of getting kicked. His mind so barbarous,
like wire throttles his being, he doesn't lift a finger.
But King mutters some days—quiet as a gentle breeze.
King say, *One day, I'll set this hell aflame.*
May something better bloom from the ash.

[Boxer]
Imagine the Negro's rage they cower from
were truly extant. Five-hundred-year behemoths welling
up inside our chests. Monstrous beings
nurtured by malice. Imagine the harm
we could cause—gleefully ceasing their reign.
Every King a Nat Turner adherent.
If we held grudges the way they fear,
nothing would remain.
Not a single bloom in the rubble.

[Boy & Dog in a Johnnypump]
King been gone for days now—his loyal hound, too.
They came in the death of night. Cat of ninetails,
manacles & fetters, arrows launched aflame. His husk
found floating gently downstream. Faithful beast a mangled
decoration. The throne rests desolate. Regicide unanswered.
A mother left in shambles. Kingdom falls
to chaos. The noble district set aflame.

[Defacement]
This land is littered with a disarray
of undone grins. Their names a swift
abstraction, a sorrow we dirge in
chorus. A reminder high above
our sullen heads: the next visage
to grace byways may well be
a novel monarch, & it will hurt
no less. Toe the line, for there is
always room amidst this plane
for the next countenance to be
unmade.

& THE REFRAIN

forgotten. trending, then forgotten. trending, then forgotten.
trending, then forgotten. trending, then forgotten. trending, then
forgotten. trending, then forgotten. trending, then forgotten.
trending, then forgotten. trending, then forgotten. trending, then
forgotten. trending, then forgotten. trending, then forgotten.
trending, then forgotten. trending, then forgotten. trending, then
forgotten. trending, then forgotten. trending, then forgotten.
trending, then forgotten. trending, then forgotten. trending, then
forgotten. trending, then forgotten. trending, then forgotten.
trending, then forgotten. trending, then forgotten. trending, then
forgotten. trending, then forgotten. trending, then forgotten.
trending, then forgotten. trending, then forgotten. trending, then
forgotten. trending, then forgotten. trending, then forgotten.
trending, then forgotten. trending, then forgotten. trending, then
forgotten. trending, then forgotten. trending, then forgotten.
trending, then forgotten. trending, then forgotten. trending, then
forgotten. trending, then forgotten. trending, then forgotten.
trending, then forgotten. trending, then forgotten. trending, then
forgotten. trending, then forgotten. trending, then forgotten.
trending, then forgotten. trending, then forgotten. trending, then
forgotten. trending, then forgotten. trending, then forgotten.
trending, then forgotten. trending, then forgotten. trending, then
forgotten. trending, then forgotten. trending, then

AMERICA MARKS EACH HUNT WITH FIREWORKS

n o f r e   e   Ahmaud Arbery Vincent M. Belmonte Breonna Taylor Eric Garner Emmett Till

w e ' l l   Angelo Crooms Sincere Pierce Marcellis Stinnette Tamir Rice Yvette Smith

n e g r o s   L Y N C H   Rayshard Brooks Carlos Carson David McAtee Philando Castile Jamar Clark

i n t h i s.   e v e r y   Charleena Chavon Lyles Fetus of Charleena Chavon Lyles George Floyd, Jr.

n a t i o n   c h i l d   o f g o o d   Trayvon Martin Winston Smith James Byrd Jr. Kenneth Chamberlain Sr.

don'tletuscatchyouprouddon'tletuscatchyouwindon'tletuscatchyouproudletuscatchyouletusletuscatchyounigg

Gregory Lloyd Edwards Chinedu Okobi David Walker, His Wife, & Their 4 Children _____

this country
only knows
how to kill
this country
only knows
how to kill
this country
only knows
how to kill
this country
only knows
how to kill
this country
only knows
how to kill
this country
only knows
how to kill
this country
only knows
how to kill
this country
only knows
how to kill
this country

mother

addict

scholar   firework

the

What   firework   **is**   father   outlaw   son

firework   firework

cost   firework

neighbor   firework   firework   daughter

firework   firework   **of**   thug   **Black?**

29

SANGUINE TEMPLE

Most days sleuthing the city I
pack a knife. Ever wary, I wait for what will
come day or night. Can't let not-
hing catch me slippin' when servants shoot.

Big-game killer for quarry like myself,
my skin precious in-
gots. Pick poised for the
harvest; excavation of a head.

Fruit of forced labor &
so many smothered dreams, I
promise they won't take me to the will-
ows willingly. Bark stripped bare by yesterday's not-
ches. The children hung from an off shoot.

Could've been myself.
Never safe, but I feel it after gin.
Elixir to exorcise the
demons dancing on my back.

This is to say I'm tired &
don't know how to not be. I
don't believe in good—cops or will.
I've known too many lamentations. My not-
ebook an elysian census; but when I hang,
I swear I didn't do it myself.

ASPIRANT DRONES

Carnivorous larvae farce war again:
militant theatrics; deft mimicry; nested wasp beetles.
How they fiend for fresh marrow, daily bread,
how the one-trick insect swarm seethes fortissimo.

Militant theatrics; wasps in the honeypot; trojan antics.
There's a pipe bomb in the sandcastle, beside the plastic spade,
& the insect swarm festers with patience, awaiting the dinner-bell bang.
Grounded in gun sounds, their carapaces thicken.

There's a pipe bomb in the honeypot, beside the toy soldiers,
watch them swarm the seashell bridge.
Grounded in gun sounds, their carapaces thicken
'til they're deadened to dissonant pleas.

I CANNOT BE YOUR MARTIN LUTHER

King, I have no rose petals for land I hatefully make a home.
Nor do I imagine each stormy morning as a brighter afternoon

aching. I cannot think these bullet-toothed beings some lonely sort,
love reverberating in their core; the trust is how they

catch you slippin', cut trajectory short, your crash site the new gospel.
I cannot hug the gunman nor break bread with taskmasters.

That's how they keep you. There's no confusing willful violence,
daily chosen sin upon this body. They sin upon this body, so I cannot

afford to call theirs love. My dreams all death-reeked, photo album
of festering, each mugshot mine. I can't stop what I didn't go pickin',

nigga—that's how we get unmade. How niggas get they fifteen
seconds of *What a shame.* Tinder-bio head-nod from white folk who

named theyself *Ally*. Each breath a mortuary-in-waiting, so hear my
violent *No.* I cannot be your King. Won't turn cheek to buckshot

or greet their hunger with sunflowers. My last act will not be
peaceful. I will not make a pretty martyr, flower wreath adorning this

twist-thicket scalp. I will not name my killer *Love*. Nor will I
for their god who made gun shops flirt with liquor stores in every

hood as if to say, *have at it!* I cannot take the high road knowing their
drones swarm above, seeking some wayward Black

with enough trust to follow their god up the on-ramp.
Never to be kettled, caught, & strung, I cannot call this love.

GOD'S GONE FISHING!

FATHER!

Now we wish
to catch a

& y
& y
& y

I've lost my sea legs. Can't keep balanced.

Shouldn't he?
Do it?

Eenie,
    Meenie,
        Miney,
            Moe,

Momma, please. Tell him I can't no more

It's okay to eat ████ *because they don't have any feelings*

Catch a rhino by the   **LIP! HAHAHAHA!**

Or was it a fish?

Isn't it lovely?
look at the water!
See how calm
Shhh!
look at the sun
see it touch the
lovely
Shhhhhh!
you're going to
scare the ███
SHHHHHHHHH!
See how calm

I've been running
or swimming
for weeks

So juicy sweet!

OOOOHH! IT'S A BIG ONE!
GOT SOME **FIGHT** TO IT!
GET IN THIS BOAT YOU
Got any hearts? UPPITY ASS ███

you're overfishing
you're overfishing
you're overfishing
you're overfishing
you're overfishing
you're overfishing
you're overfishing
you're overfishing
you're overfishing
you're overfishing

UNCLE!

Teach a man to fish **& WON'T BE NONE, NIGGA!**

Do what
    alabaster daddies
        always do?

Go fish!

Wait, where'd the lovely go?

God's not finished

ONCE THE KINGDOM HAS FALLEN

I'll lay down / this crown / on the side of the road / alone / maybe /
or surrounded / by salivating canines / with gleaming teeth / or wild
boars / left untethered so long / they feral & quick / to gore guts / of
whomever is / in the wrong neck / of the hood / overgrown / with
dense foliage / splitting concrete / putting mankind's many wonders /
to shame / how quick we become / a memory / how swift this / world
is to purge / itself of illness / of us / & when I do rest / this heavy /
head / my neck will wail / its sorrow / or relief / maybe / I'll let
the earth / do with me / what it will / when / there's nothing / left to
fight for / I too will rush / to become / undone / & there will be no
one / left / to pray for me / to light my way / to whichever circle / is
mine to claim / & if you find me / rotting / in the street / there was no
sense / in my passing / nor in staining / the pavement / our massive
memory / final tomb / with tears / simply leave me / there / to nurture
the beasts in need / of sustenance / maybe / pour some out / maybe /
on me / & light my festering aflame / leave me something / intricate /
adorning / what once was / maybe / watch me / become a memory /
overgrown / & splitting at the seams

AT EIGHT-YEARS-OLD, I OUTRAN A BOY WHO SURELY WANTED ME DEAD

What can be said for the boy with a stick
running down squirrels because he can?

Running down a squirrel because
it can't fight something so massive.

Can't fight something so massive—
the weight of caged-hound hunger.

The weight of metal pipe in hand,
chasing Black boys who play with dolls—

Black boy whose dolls scrap better.
Boy so sissy; he can't fight something so massive.

Massive as the boy with the pipe
who's never been stranger to fists—their weight.

No stranger to fists—their weight.
What can be said for the boy with a stick?

STUBBORN BUCK

Pulling the trigger was easy enough, & I
        didn't mind hauling the harvest. Nor
the stink. Nor the mess. I didn't mind

        following the splatter
to find the collapsed kill.
If you stayed, I would tell you

there's just one part, dear—
        it nearly broke me—see, the shot punctured
a lung; it's why he suffered

        so long. How he fled for a time.
& when I hoisted his body
to harvest a life,

the Texan breeze blew
        through the foreign opening;
his lungs filled again.

        & hours after passing,
the dead moaned softly,
        & hours after passing,
I could swear he was still in pain.

FLASHBACK TO THE SMOKING GUN
For M.B.

to the campus we could never afford but crept through sometimes,
not on nothing nefarious, just hooping with a cousin

& his friends & some boys who been spoon-fed
since they was twinkles in an iris. I recall like yesterday's

refuse the way them White boys watched you climb so high
above their heads, just to shove you down at the peak.

I remember perfectly the way you shot up in a flash, ready
to stand ground & then some. How I stopped you,

grabbed hold with every ounce of conviction I could muster,
said, *Homie, look around. These boys will sue us out our socks,*

if luck is on our side. & perhaps there was too much fever in my
vigilance, but I refused to lose you. Refused to read an article ending

with officer; narrative expurgating your name. I remember, through
just rage, you seemed to hear the somber wisdom in my words.

You relented, & we continued the game, shoulders heavy with
assorted chips. White boys grinned, still silver-ladened lips,

as you limped to get back on defense. Remember what happened
next? I do, a bit—still recall the second shove, the third,

the moment you hit the ground. The moment I discovered
what it was to be wrothful, how I dove like a prey-bird,

seeking the throats of penny-tongued poachers. How I needed each
cubic inch of smoke, & it took a great deal of mediation

to keep me from evening the score—for a moment, logic &
consequences were trifling things. All I knew for certain

were those posh perpetual pups, who never scuffed paws for shit,
thought to put hands on the man who was perhaps my only friend.

I didn't think of how we shouldn't be there—
security lazing 'round the alcove,

nor how quick it goes from sound scuffle to operator & body bags—
I remember you rose to your feet, muttering, *my nigga*.

& proceeded to behemoth through the paint
'til the sun got sick of spectating.

How we kept it hoops the remaining duration,
how they never, *ever*, put a hand on you again.

WHEN ABOUT

I try to keep a few loose dollars in case someone is needing
warm coffee on a blistery winter morning or whatever

worship their temple trills for—it's not my business to question
their refuge. But in truth, I save my capital mostly for motherland folk

far from home, hunted like the holiest grail, golden goose, wounded rook;
I keep a cache on hand for whomever knows this nation's nip,

mahogany chapped by persistent bland we call, not-home, but close enough.
For those who had the deck stacked far from reach—never got to play

their hand or sit in gawdy casino chairs fondling a watery margarita.
This is not to paint me great & giving—I'm mostly just anxious &

daydreamy enough to wonder, *what if this were me,*
or a homie with no respite left from all the biting

cold. All this tundra has to offer. & one day, I was biking
home, counting falling flakes as I went, whimsical as you please,

when, wonder-drunk as I was, I nearly ran a red, nearly
clogged an artery of death machines blaring, swift, & careless.

& with the quick of one who has known death's presence too often,
I slammed my brakes, trusted tire studs to bite ice enough

to keep from gliding to an early end. & they did,
& when I calmed enough to glance, I had stopped beside a man

with skin more sun-blessed than mine, hoping to uncover enough
god in America to rest his weary bones. The frost held steadfast.

I searched for my few dollars but I was ass-out.
I fingered two gold chains dangling from my neck,

their weight against my clavicle; I figured they might barter well.
Might fill a stomach, perhaps afford a place to lie low. The gold I copped

at first influx of funds. A little dream dreamt since childhood, since music
videos on BET rolling 24/7, back before Chicago's son sold his soul

for a fresh necklace, & T.I.'s hat was still *way* back, maybe reaching for
brighter days, for sunlight, or enough god in America. Back when

there was no cash for tropical trips, car gifts, or afterschool skiing. Back
when Momma worked her hands to the bone making up for what wasn't

around. & I saw this man who was needing, & thought to give
my shallow claim a new home. Thought, surely, I don't need both.

& when the traffic light blared green, the cars behind me
screamed a mighty fury, & I pushed down on my pedals,

bidding both greetings & farewell with a wave to
the man I cared enough about to notice, but not enough

to part with an ounce of status. Not enough to walk naked-necked,
gold passed on for the love of my fellow man, trying just to live.

LET ME BE CLEAR—I'M AFRAID

of the cutting cold whistling through open pores,
the silence of sliding through fresh fallen snow
or shifting in a car seat, to better say
goodbye as some angsty heartbreak
oozes through speakers at the right-wrong
moment. Forlorn sighs & retracing breath
beyond the fall. It's strange
how little cities fill with distant
folk who sometimes slide for love, sometimes
slide for survival, that *can't do another winter
alone again.* It's strange
how we slide together & fro,
leaving imprints on unsullied snow.
Pulling & shoving as the sun dips
& swells. *Again.*
It's strange. How we take
to fill what's missing, how
we've mastered the art of goodbye.
Knowing no catch to release, no slippin'
when we slide. I'm afraid of the quiet
cold that stalks a curt farewell.
I'd rather the whole world stop—rather glide off fresh fallen
Love. Pardon, I'm afraid I'm late for a meeting.
I'm planning to leave
again.

SCRAWLED ACROSS THE WALL OF A COLLEGE BAR BATHROOM: *DON'T DATE RAPPERS.*

& listen, I don't know many

      folks who tried but I hear it ends a mangled mess.

        I hear love don't mix

      with all that ego. I hear it tastes sweet

as a nosebleed in the end, relational backwash

      thick with sediment. All that ego

        makes me wonder if there aren't such

      warning labels for poets—

& I know, I know, there I go making everything

      about me again. But listen, what is a poet

        but a rapper without stage presence?

      All brooding reservation, yet, somehow not hurting

for ego, & listen, I know how hard I am to love;

      how quickly I make footfalls

        when hurt swaggers forth. How I learned

      to vanish from the best of 'em.

How I dip when specters of sleepy Sundays

spent intertwined with another

come creeping along the periphery.

& lost in all this fitful reminiscing,

I fear I've grown accustomed to prints left in snow,

dinners in solitude. Self-reliant & safe

with few reasons to giggle or burden

my friends, who too grow fewer by the hour.

& leaving the bathroom, & the bar, I wander,

wallowing in lonely as the day grows bashful,

following a frigid river to a bridge,

desolate as myself, & snow falls now,

sweetening my midnight beard,

adorning the mostly frozen surface below.

& looking back, there's one set of tracks

for as far as the eye can see, & heaven eclipses sod

with renewed vigor, & I can't help but wonder,

alone on this bridge, who I think I am

to harbor all this ego. Who I think I am

to leave nothing but footprints & crestfallen loves.

(UP)ROOTED

At the wedding, Uncle told me of the
trees which blacken by the day. He told me
they were sick; were fighting off a plague &
wilting by the grove. Said no one knows a
way to keep them useful, so instead, we
split them sideways, ripping root from soil
swaths denuded by the hour, endless
plains embellished by cadavers. Brushing
bark made sweeter, hand an off-black berry,
sickly scents came lunging for the lively
drunken man. I offered them my essence,
down from cheek to soil knowing nation's
nip. Gods brought low like Locke, Castile,
Floyd, & Winston. Kings eclipsed.

We watch the light ebb.

TARTARUS

After Jean-Michel Basquiat

[Maid in Olympia]
When the next King is birthed, it'll be feet-first
into a party's chase. When the next is known, they'll be
quarried like King. Brought to know such sorrow,
& the sunrise dwelling betwixt. There is
nothing so fierce as a Black woman's love. For she knows
too well what horrors lurk in tall brush. Salivating
for a heaping taste of ichor.

[La Hara]
See they made of marrow & armaments,
bloodshot & thirsting for excess.
Such decadence littering the unkempt
concrete. Melanin memory muddling the beat.
See they chins dripping with pride. Wild
beasts fiending for fresh marks. Ain't they
perfect Robocops? Pristine? Watch them
paint the whole hood red.

[Acidquiat]
King's dead. A bloody mess of viscera.
Said to have went down grinning, content
to meet his nettle-fingered killer with a warmth
so radiant one can't help but wither. & yet,
King splattered all the same, his mind beside
the shattered crown. His smile wiped clean-slate.

[Back of Neck]
Regal bodies are a novelty—ripped asunder
& sent like love notes betwixt the resting
mob. A shriveled heart to revel in the
hunt, some vertebrae to craft a quirky
carcanet, garlands of twisted viscera
just because it's nice. The rest they leave
rotting in the street. Funeral fit for a King.

[Untitled—Yellow Bone King]
Don't sleep on King.
His grave was cut too shallow. Loam easily muddled.
King ain't dropped so easy, no god-kin meant to perish.
He roams now the countryside, crown made whole again.
Needs no regiment to handle light work. He'll bludgeon his
killers a bloody mess, flailing a dislodged femur.
His body made to shamble—grin made whole again.

[The Ring]
Devil a bad man they say, often wroth & barbarous;
but ain't we flame-keepers, too? Ain't his children try
to break us down for hunnids? This place is brimful-handed,
hath no clue how to quell such resistance. See us rise,
day or night, our nappy heads held high.
Ogun's spear shimmers overhead. A croon turnt battle cry.

[Boom for Real]
& then the city came to life. All of its strongholds
assembled thorned wire & chains hastily,
amalgamating to a skull-faced behemoth. Its hollow-
eyed holiness raged in unlit alleyways. The tanks,
drones, & ghetto birds divided the city
with a thin blue brush.
& yet, it all burned the same.

[History of Black People]
My people are more than upraised arms. Much more
than perforated things. Our sorrows extensive but
hardly without end. We royalty in so many
languages—varied trappings of godhood.
But like each religion which ever once was,
we're different depictions of the same
sort of holy. Thousands of Kings.
Countless ways to say *sunrise.*

AMERICAN-GODS

There's an ancient American chant
which wildfired 'round the globe.
I forget how it's said, how the tongue curls or lips purse,
if it favors a hard "R." How mouths meant for taste
& passion turn to a shooting range. I forget
the specific imagery, but the gist is this:

Only thing a nigga loves
more than liquor
is hip-hop. that loud
loud big-lipped
noise, that's all
it is, you know.
Noise. It's all loud,
all sounds the same.
All fast cars, ego,
& money. & big,
loud, gaudy gilded
chains. Why do they
still wear chains?
Big loud uppity niggas,
big loud uppity hip-hop—
I hate that.
Why can't they just
be humble? I mean,
why can't they shut
their goddamned mouths
for a second?

*

American-Gods   noun
Amer·i·can- ' gäds | \ə-'mer-ə-kən-' gäds
Definition of American-Gods (Entry 1 of 1)
1 : SUM LOUD ASS NIGGAS

*

BIG LOUD NIGGAS!

WITH BIG LOUD GOLD!

LINKED TO UNITY

FORMING A CHAIN,

SACRED THING,

OR MAYBE A MOLD

FOR TEETH!

GOLD FOR TEETH!

NOSES, TOO!

HOOP EARRINGS!

TITANS DRIPPING!

THE EARTH GILDED

WITH SIREN SONGS

OF BIG LOUD NIGGAS!

LOUD NIGGAS WHO

MADE IT OUT THE MUD

OR DIDN'T NEED TO

& CAME OUT SHINING!

BUT LOUD
                    & NIGGAS
                              ALL THE SAME!

& WATCH THE NON-DEIFIED,

THEIR SKIN SWELLING

TO CRIMSON HUES

HEARING US CARRY ON

SINGING SONGS THAT

WAS NEVER MEANT TO

INVADE THEIR SUBURBAN

LIFESTYLINGS!

BIG LOUD NIGGAS!

WHO SOMETIMES SPEAK CURSIVE?

BEAUTIFUL SOUNDS

TO BIG LOUD BEATS!

BIG LOUD NIGGAS

WHO LEFT ONE TRAP

FOR ANOTHER!

REFUSING TO

BRAGGADOCIOUS

BEATS SO LOUD,

BUMPING COLE,

WHIP MIGHT BLOW!

LIKE A GODDAMNED

ON THE NEWS

BIG LOUD NIGGAS

BE CONTAINED!

FOR THE CULTURE!

A CADILLAC ROLLED BY

& IT SOUNDED LIKE THE

RATTLING! SHAKING!

HURRICANE! LIKE A RAPPER

FIXING HIS LIPS TO SAY

THE PRESIDENT HATES BIG LOUD NIGGAS!

THE SONG BOUNCED

BUILDINGS TO A

CRACKED & UNKEMPT

WHO DROPPED THEIR BALLS,

ELBOWS & SHOTS

TO THE SOUND

WHO MADE IT!

ALL ALONG THE NEARBY

BASKETBALL COURT

& FULL OF YOUNG NIGGAS

LEFT THEIR TOSSING OF

TO DANCE UNBURDENED

OF BIG LOUD NIGGAS!

NEVER TO BE CONTAINED!

TO WHOM IT MAY CONCERN

After Danez Smith

I've left earth in search of darker depths, waters so murky
I could thrive a lifetime with none wiser. Spelunking crescent-deep
beneath Guam. Hanging with anglerfish & pressure so steady
it burdens like home. Not so much the terrors come, just enough
to spawn a smirk. Eight tons-per-inch a petty sum to Suns thought
novaed at a bang. No weight too grand for us with nations on our
backs. Umber Atlas on bended knee, hoisting culture & country
without waver, finessing godlike burdens while watching for swelling
torchlight—ravens conspiring above. I've left Earth in search of
shelter; some breathing room to commune with salt-lunged siblings.
I've left no trace nor trail but prints along the shore, they too will
vanish in the tide. Rising and falling swift as empires, leaving nothing
but eroded ground. I can't stand your ground—how its grasses grow
off spilled blood. How each blade bears an engraving: *Floyd, Byrd,
Garner, Rice.* How each pyre burns with bundles of excuses. I'm sick
of your excuses. Your children singing a chorus of *buts*, preaching to
the wake, all the ways we had it coming. Shushing the mother who
sobs over an open casket, praying her sorrow might grow a kid back.
No, I will not settle nor pipe down. I do not wish to behave. Color me
radical if it gives you cause, I'm only searching for breath untainted
by iron. I'm searching for breath with all my kinfolk & you would
name it terror. We can't grocery shop without stepping over bodies,
yet you would speak of fright. Your ever-shaking knees, America the
fearful, all chattering teeth for Black boys smiling outside the corner
store, shit-talking and slap-boxing over a fistful of Mike & Ikes.
Because you know some stains don't wash fully. Because the water
dun' faded crimson to turmeric. Because my cousin's ichor is still
caked beneath your fingernails as you reach a hand in 'friendship.'
Because everyone knows you have no want for friendship. Because
that would name us equal. Because that would deem us worthy, &
then what would be made of all our fallen?
I've left Earth for a life beneath the wake. Some place dark as night &
free of white-donned choirs. I'm swimming with my ancestors in a

jungle of jellyfish. I am not coming back. I leave you your blood-soaked state. I leave you your pitchy choir, who competes with the trill of your machinations coming home to crumble. I'm building a citadel on the ocean's floor, among unnamed leviathans, I bid my siblings join me. I bid my people leave you to your writhing. We'll forge a sanctuary in waters so Black you'll never follow. Waters so Black you'd name it night terror; so Black our children come home.

So Black we call it home.

HOW WE HUNT

Ain't it silly? How we toil
day & night? Callused hands
cramp for such uncertainty. Ever
the beaver bustling, making dam-
nation, a wall of sticks
meant to stop tsunamis. So
impractical how we hunt
sunken chests with no promise
of glittering insides. Ever seaside
shoveling, cracking clams, we oughta
slow down. Enjoy the song
the ocean sings. Relish
the last breaths
of a planet. The sweetest
death rattle never heard.

EYE OF THE BIVOUAC

It aches to know something worth reaching for.
Or someone. It's silly how hearts find a way
to cartwheel even as Earth becomes a mortuary,

a murder of butterflies run amok in my gut. I'm sorry
if I don't make sense. I'm caught up in the moment,
trying to find the mastermind who shattered their terrarium,

planted milkweed in my being to ensure they outstay
their welcome—such famished & beady-eyed bodyguests.
A million monarchs aerobating, skyline a heart-like flutter.

I'm coming to grips with this dawning. I've battened down the hatches—
ship flounders all the same, captain's cabin asquirm. Tip of the
hurricane. A cyclone-in-waiting, how my core knows to tick again.

How it quickens when she's near, rat-a-tating faster than Lil Vert's uzi,
how it melancholies when she's missing overlong. I swore I swore off
such luditude, pardon, latitude—the storm chase to see her again.

I'm not a man who went looking to dote. I'm a stubborn child
who thought he could outpace a tempest. But ain't them thangs track stars?
Don't they leave nothing in their wake but dumbstruck castaways?

I promise this is not a love poem. I'm far too timorous to use that term,
my sea legs much too shaky. I sailed a great voyage, went a great bout,
but come the gloaming, it was never my place to shadow the swarm.

Lost in a storm of forewings the moment she said hello.

I DON'T DANCE

but I'd die to frolic on this nation's writhing
ruins. Caste brought low, swapped with liberation
promised from birth, prisons desolate, my folks
brought back to gem-touched living. Back
choosing fates, chasing passions outside,
without fear of gettin' buckshot waiting for a mule,
no concrete left to jungle or blue-suited killers,
no pipelines in schools or land, in fact, no land
to break & border. Just rolling plains & modest
domiciles crafted from communal wealth which
lessens as we need. In fact, no people need.
No 9-to-5 to get by on ramen noodles, no slavening
bread bandits, no chopping of hands. Activists don't
vanish in window-tinted vans. Only mass graves
belong to guns & deadened weapons.
& no elder sits their child down to talk on nothin'
but lovin'. & Black boys need not harden,
can walk outside hood-donned,
sagging, well-locked, & carefree. Never followed
at the shop. No shops. No property. No gods, no kings,
no slavers, or ballistic whips. I'd live to know a land of
care where one could frolic nude-footed without
stepping on someone's broken bliss, where one could
dip legs in lakes & linger without fear of what creeps
around the bend. A place I could contemplate
making a kid without a pang of dread. Without visions
of small bodies dotting willows. Sun setting some scarlet hue
as helicopters chop overhead.

I don't dance, but I long to watch the revelry
from afar, see so many brown bodies
shimmy more than sway, bounce more than drop,
bop more than fade away. The elders all huddled
with frost-ladened liquors, sobbing disbelief,
& the children not knowing why.

PREVIOUSLY PUBLISHED

Sarah Rising. Beaming Books. Minneapolis, MN. 2022.

A Door Made for Me. (Written with Tyler Merritt.) Hachette Book Group. New York, NY. 2022.

Looking for Happy. Beaming Books. Minneapolis, MN. 2023.

NOTES

"God Say is an Eintou," a poetic form created by African American poets as a protest against White cultural traditions of poetry, and what was considered *literary,* The form is often used to spread wisdom.

"Tartarus is a Pecha Kucha," a form created by Terrence Hayes. It was written after multiple artworks by Jean-Michel Basquiat; each micro poem is named after the artwork that inspired it.

"[Dad] Had Four Kids, three of Which Were Precious," is a blackout poem, crafted from my late father's obituary.

"Sanguine Temple is a Golden Shovel," another form created by Terrence Hayes. The last word in each line is taken from the Jericho Brown poem, *Bullet Points.*

While it is not written after any particular poem, "What Color Was the Rhino" was greatly inspired by Douglas Kearney's exceptional visual poetry.

"To Whom It May Concern" was written after Danez Smith's timeless poem, *Dear White America.*

ACKNOWLEDGMENTS

Big thanks to the entire team at Button Poetry for seeing the vision, & to my editor Simone Person, who helped make sense of a particularly messy first draft.

To my many artistic homes, including: Monkeybear's Harmolodic Workshop, The Loft Literary Center, Open Eye Figure Theatre, & Vermont College of Fine Arts—& the incredible faculty who have pushed me, taught me, & offered new connections.

To the poets who have directly inspired my work: Hanif Abdurraqib, Jericho Brown, Ross Gay, Terrance Hayes, Douglas Kearney, Ada Limón, Shane McCrae, Bao Phi, & Danez Smith.

An immense thank you to the mentors & fellow artists who helped me elevate my craft & learn to believe in my work: William Alexander, Peter Geye, Molly Beth Griffin, Gretchen Marquette, Chris Santiago, Sun Yung Shin, & Danez Smith.

& To my ever-expanding community of artists, the folks who lift me up when I stumble, remind me why I write, & inspire me to be a better human & community member: Ann Cardinal, John Coy, Dr. Sarah Park Dahlen, Michael Kleber-Diggs, Molly Beth Griffin, Terry Horstman, Douglas Kearney, Morgan LaRocca, Tyler Merritt, Bao Phi, Ollie Schminkey, Taiwana Shambley, Stephen Shaskan, Trisha SpeedShaskan, Oanh Vu, Liping Vong, Saymoukda Vongsay, Lizz Windnagle, & Andrew Young.

A big thanks to my very first writing group, with whom I commiserate, grow, & constantly goof: Rita Feinstein & Sarah Fowerbaugh.

& To my irreplaceable "Women in STEM" who have remained an anchoring presence throughout grad school & wrapping up this collection. The privilege of calling y'all my friends is a daily delight: Kauakanilehua Adams, Caroline Cullinane, & Mary Neville.

To my dear friend Ari Tison, who inspires me to no end, & is a most treasured collaborator.

To my dear friend & literary agent, Savannah Brooks, to whom I owe my career. A second thank you, for emphasis, & for always meeting my moments of overwhelming anxiety with patience & grace.

To my booking agent, Sarah DeVore, for helping me navigate a whole new world of gigs & accommodations.

To my brothers, without whom I would not be breathing: Manzi Bagurusi & Geoffrey Gill.

To the wonderful Circus of Fools who introduced me to the world of Faerun, & remain a bi-weekly source of laughter, support, friendship, & inspiration.

To all my friends & supporters who are too many to name, but without whom I certainly would not be the person I am today. To the friends who are no longer friends, (sincerely,) for once playing a large role in my life.

A heartfelt thank you to my haters & doubters. You too make me great.

Thank you to the family who claimed me when not everyone would— who made me feel loved & at home in the lone star state, & whom I love eternally.

A sincere thank you to my father, who taught me much from afar.

The biggest thanks of all to my mother who did a damn fine job raising me, while working her ass off & chasing her own ambitions. Whose endless care & support imbued in me the confidence to chase my goals with abandon.

& of course, thank you, dearest reader, for going on this journey with me. Thank you for honoring me, & these poems, with your time.

Thank you to the following literary journals who published previous versions of these poems:

Allium: *"Believe What I Say"* & *"In Minneapolis"*

Water~Stone: *"Philophobia: An Heirloom"* & *"Pantheon."*

The Under Review: *"Flashback to the Smoking Gun"*

ABOUT THE AUTHOR

Ty Chapman is the author of SARAH RISING (Beaming 2022); A DOOR MADE FOR ME, written with Tyler Merritt (WorthyKids 2022); LOOKING FOR HAPPY (Beaming 2023); TARTARUS (Button Poetry 2024); as well as multiple forthcoming children's books through various publishers.

Ty was a finalist for Tin House's 2022 Fall Residency, Button Poetry's 2020 Chapbook Contest, and Frontier Magazine's New Voices Contest.

He is currently an MFA candidate in creative writing for children and young adults at Vermont College of Fine Arts and was recently named a Loft Literary Center Mirrors & Windows fellow and Mentor Series fellow.

AUTHOR BOOK RECOMMENDATIONS

Black Movie by Danez Smith

Black Movie is an incredible collection of poems. Its subject matter is unfortunately ever-relevant; thankfully the voice and range of emotions the speaker communicates with are likewise everlasting. In many ways, this was the collection that taught me the power of a poem.

The Crown Ain't Worth Much by Hanif Abdurraqib

A gorgeous collection which flits from grand subjects like gentrifi-
cation and the Black experience, to deeply granular and intimate
poems more concerned with the personal. This collection is a
masterclass on vulnerability, paired with haunting imagery and an
unforgettable voice.

BUTTON POETRY BEST SELLERS

Neil Hilborn, *Our Numbered Days*
Hanif Abdurraqib, *The Crown Ain't Worth Much*
Sabrina Benaim, *Depression & Other Magic Tricks*
Rudy Francisco, *Helium*
Rachel Wiley, *Nothing Is Okay*
Neil Hilborn, *The Future*
Phil Kaye, *Date & Time*
Andrea Gibson, *Lord of the Butterflies*
Blythe Baird, *If My Body Could Speak*
Andrea Gibson, *You Better Be Lightning*

Available at buttonpoetry.com/shop and more!

OTHER BOOKS BY BUTTON POETRY

If you enjoyed this book, please consider checking out some of our others, below. Readers like you allow us to keep broadcasting and publishing. Thank you!

Desireé Dallagiacomo, *SINK*
Dave Harris, *Patricide*
Michael Lee, *The Only Worlds We Know*
Raych Jackson, *Even the Saints Audition*
Brenna Twohy, *Swallowtail*
Porsha Olayiwola, *i shimmer sometimes, too*
Jared Singer, *Forgive Yourself These Tiny Acts of Self-Destruction*
Adam Falkner, *The Willies*
George Abraham, *Birthright*
Omar Holmon, *We Were All Someone Else Yesterday*
Rachel Wiley, *Fat Girl Finishing School*
Bianca Phipps, *crown noble*
Natasha T. Miller, *Butcher*
Kevin Kantor, *Please Come Off-Book*
Ollie Schminkey, *Dead Dad Jokes*
Reagan Myers, *Afterwards*
L.E. Bowman, *What I Learned From the Trees*
Patrick Roche, *A Socially Acceptable Breakdown*
Rachel Wiley, *Revenge Body*
Ebony Stewart, *BloodFresh*
Ebony Stewart, *Home.Girl.Hood.*
Kyle Tran Mhyre, *Not A Lot of Reasons to Sing, but Enough*
Steven Willis, *A Peculiar People*
Topaz Winters, *So, Stranger*
Darius Simpson, *Never Catch Me*
Blythe Baird, *Sweet, Young, & Worried*
Siaara Freeman, *Urbanshee*
Robert Wood Lynn, *How to Maintain Eye Contact*
Junious 'Jay' Ward, *Composition*
Usman Hameedi, *Staying Right Here*
Sean Patrick Mulroy, *Hated for the Gods*
Sierra DeMulder, *Ephemera*
Taylor Mali, *Poetry By Chance*
Matt Coonan, *Toy Gun*
Matt Mason, *Rock Stars*
Rudy Francisco, *Excuse Me As I Kiss The Sky*
Miya Coleman, *Cottonmouth*

Available at buttonpoetry.com/shop and more!